THE WILD Thornberrys™

SURVIVAL GUIDE

Based on the TV series *The Wild Thornberrys*® created by Klasky Csupo, Inc.
as seen on Nickelodeon®

ISBN 0-439-17963-7

12 11 10 9 8 7 6 5 4 3 2 1   0 1 2 3 4 5/0

Printed in the U S A

First Scholastic printing, May 2000

Designed by Giuseppe Castellano

The WILD Thornberrys™

SURVIVAL GUIDE

by Adam Beechen

SCHOLASTIC INC.

New York   Toronto   London   Auckland   Sydney
Mexico City   New Delhi   Hong Kong

TABLE OF CONTENTS

Hi! I'm Eliza Thornberry, and I'm just like any twelve-year-old, except that I travel all over the world with my family, helping them make nature documentaries. And I can talk to animals. But that's a secret, so please don't tell!

We've learned a lot of things during our travels to far-off places—what to do and what not to do. It's all written in this book, so wherever you go, this guide might just come in handy.

IN GOOD COMPANY

It's really important to know who's on your trip with you. I travel with my family. Let me introduce them.

Here's my dad, Nigel. He's an expert on everything in nature—so he's helpful to have on a trip. He knows all about rare birds, the jungles of Burma, and why you shouldn't eat those red berries with the white spots!

This is my mom, Marianne. She's a filmmaker and editor. She and Dad work together on his show, *Nigel Thornberry's Animal World*. And she still finds time to take care of all of us!

7

Debbie is my sixteen-year-old sister. If the jungle had shopping malls, she'd love it! She says nature's not cool, but I know she has a better time than she says she does!

Darwin is a chimpanzee and he's my best friend. He'd rather stay at camp and eat Cheese Treats all day than hang out with a crocodile, or hunt with a tiger, but he's always there whenever—and wherever—I need him!

We found Donnie in the jungle, and now he lives with us! He's hard to keep up with, and we can't understand what he's saying, but he really seems to like being with us!

WHERE HAVE YOU BEEN.

It's a good idea to keep a journal so you can remember the things you've seen—and what to avoid on your next visit. I've been to lots of places, so my journal's pretty full. Take a look!

EPAL

Cold and snowy, with lots of mountains. Saw a few snow leopards. Met the Abominable Snowman. He's not all that abominable. In fact, he was

GREAT BARRIER REEF

Runs along the coast of Australia. All kinds of plants and coral and fish live there. But watch out for the sharks. One shark tried to chow down on dad's foot!

AFRICAN SAVANNA

Flat and grassy. Animals form herds to protect each other from lions. Met a giraffe who kept a lookout for other animals while they drank. Tried to help the giraffe do his job, but it's definitely easier when you have a really long ck!

GALÁPAGOS ISLANDS

Rocky and hot. Formed by volcanoes years and years ago. Tortoises and birds and all kinds of things live here now, even if the volcanoes still erupt once in a while. Note: Get a long way away before the volcanoes erupt!

AMAZON RAIN FOREST

Dark and green, with tons of colorful animals. A bunch of jaguars thought I was a princess! Found a hidden temple no one's seen for years!

THE COMMVEE:
INSIDE AND OUT

We travel from place to place in our Commvee, which is sort of a combination mobile home and film studio. It's got everything we need to feel comfy—and safe—no matter where we go!

Our control panel keeps the Commvee safe in snowstorms, floods, even earthquakes and stampedes!

When I'm not using my bed, it folds up into a couch.

My Mom does her film editing in the Commvee. Donnie's not allowed to go near her equipment, no matter what! Of course, that hardly ever stops him. . . .

There are storage compartments all over the Commvee. Some of them hold Mom's film and lights. Others are where Debbie keeps her collection of *Teenage Wasteland* magazines. And one compartment is filled with Darwin's Cheese Treats.

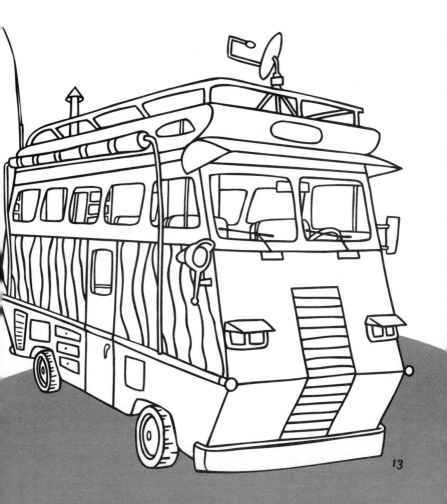

YOU'VE GOTTA HAVE THESE

Are YOU living out of the back of a Commvee, a million billion miles from anything civilized, like a fast food restaurant, or a video store?

Do YOU wonder how you can stay hip and trendy when your parents totally oppress you by dragging you around the world?

Of course you don't, because no one else has a life as weird as mine. But I've learned to cope! If your family's making you vacation in the middle of nowhere, you better get these things:

• A subscription to *Teenage Wasteland* magazine: It's my only link to all the really cool things in life—boys, music, fashion, makeup . . . um, did I say boys?

• A short wave radio: It's absolutely essential if you want to hear "Teenage Angst," the new single from Des Brodean.

• A good supply of suntan lotion: We're always going somewhere hot and sunny. I may not have a lot of friends my own age, dates, or my own room, but I do have a killer tan!

• Lots and lots of bubble gum: It can get boring looking at rhinos, wombats, condors, and dugongs all the time. But I always have a good time blowing bubbles and snapping my gum!

• A lot of waterproof makeup: Because it can get sweaty in the jungle. And I never know when I might fall into a crocodile-infested stream. Or when Donnie might pour an entire six-pack of soda over my head. Or when I might break into tears of joy when I hear that Des Brodean will be playing a concert in Senegal!

GETTING THROUGH CUSTOMS

Sometimes, people in other countries do things that might seem strange to you. But those are their customs, and if you know what they are, it might help you understand them!

• In India, people believe cows are sacred and let them do whatever they want. If a cow lies down in the middle of a busy street, no one tries to move it. They will wait for the cow to move on on its own!

• Masai warriors aren't allowed to drink milk in their parents' tents. I wonder if Eliza thinks she's a real Masai. We have a hard time getting her to drink her milk!

• In Egypt, when a man wants to marry a woman, the groom's entire family proposes to her. That's a good way to get to know your in-laws!

• A Bedouin nomad wears headgear made from cloth and rope, which tells you how important the man is in the tribe. Hmm . . . what rank does a bandanna have?

• Men of the Dinka tribe in Africa try to outjump each other to impress the women of the tribe. Personally, I always prefer flowers!

THE EXPLORER'S BACKPACK

When Darwin and I go exploring in the jungle, we always try to be prepared!

But Eliza, it's hard to be prepared when we run into something we weren't expecting—which happens almost every time!

Since you never know what you'll find in the wild, it's a good idea to have certain things in your backpack wherever you go—like a compass! If you have one of these, you'll always know which direction you're headed.

Or a bag of Cheese Treats! It's good to have something tasty to snack on when you're on a long hike!

Bring a poncho! They don't call it the rain forest for nothing!

And don't forget the bug spray! You may not be happy to see them, but mosquitoes, gnats, and other creepy, crawly things will always be happy to see—and bite—you!

You'll also need a whistle! If you get lost in the jungle, it'll let people know where you are!

Did I mention that you should bring Cheese Treats?

ANIMAL FACTS

I've learned many an unusual fact about animals in my days as a naturalist. Why, I'll bet you didn't know these tantalizing—and important—tidbits!

• The lyrebird can copy many sounds, from the way you and I talk, to a train whistle!

• Sailors used to mistake Australian dugongs, or sea cows, for mermaids. That's quite the giggle, if you've ever seen a sea cow up close!

• In winter, stoats not only change their color from brown to white, they change their name, too! In colder months, stoats are known as ermine.

• The anaconda is the world's largest snake, and can survive for months—and sometimes years—without food. I don't know what I'd do if I had to go without my kippers for that long!

• Gray kangaroos can jump as far as forty-four feet. I only jumped that far once, when I accidentally fell off a cliff into some soft bushes!

• Polar bears can smell their dinners from as far as twenty miles away. And people say things about MY nose!

• Zebra stripes and giraffe coats are like human fingerprints. No two patterns are the same!

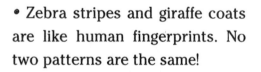

• Wombats need to be chewing on something all the time, or else their teeth grow like the grass on the Wimbledon tennis court!

• Only chimpanzees and humans can recognize themselves in mirrors.

• Elephants can be trained to do a hundred different things at the mere tap of a stick on different parts of their bodies. Astounding!

WATCH YOUR LANGUAGE!

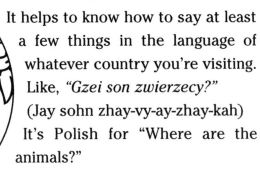

It helps to know how to say at least a few things in the language of whatever country you're visiting. Like, *"Gzei son zwierzecy?"* (Jay sohn zhay-vy-ay-zhay-kah) It's Polish for "Where are the animals?"

One of the most important phrases is *"Hvor er posthus?"* (For air post'-hoos?) It's Danish for "Where's the post office?"

Say *"Matata matata!"*
That's Swahili for "Whatever!"

I know how to say "Do you have any kippers?" in many languages.
In Japanese, it's *"Anatawa sakana wo motte imasuka?"*
(Ah-nah'-ta-wa sah-kah'-nah-wo moh-tay e-ma-su'-kah?)

"Eee eee eee AAH aah aah eee EEE!"
That's Chimpanzee for "Don't touch my Cheese Treats!"

KNOW YOUR HUMANS

Don't get me wrong, Eliza is my best friend, and her family is very nice to me, but even so, it's *not* always easy to live with humans. They can be awfully uncivilized! Fortunately, I've learned a few lessons that make traveling with them much easier.

• Always find a secret, safe storage place for your Cheese Treats! You never know when a certain little boy with messy hair might decide to go tearing through your things!

• Humans LOVE to explore. If you're exploring with them in a tree, be prepared to catch them because they have a habit of falling—especially Eliza!

• Never practice your screeching when someone's making dinner—unless you want to be eating that dinner off the walls and floor!

• Most humans like to groom themselves, so don't worry about picking bugs out of their hair. Of course, it can be fun to put bugs *in* Debbie's hair—they make her jump around like a kangaroo!

• When traveling with a girl who happens to want to chat with some tigers in the middle of their hunt, it's fine if you happen to remember an appointment with your veterinarian that you just can't miss!

ANIMAL CHATTER

I've made a lot of new friends since I received my special powers to talk to animals. Some animals are easy to talk to, but some have other things on their minds! Here's who to look out for:

• Tortoises on the Galápagos Islands speak v-e-r-y s-l-o-w-l-y, and some are so old, they don't hear very well. You have to be really patient with them—rushing them will get you nowhere!

• Don't even try having a conversation with a Komodo dragon. They're so mean, they're not interested in making friends, just in making you their lunch!

• I have a koala pal from Australia named Bim. It's best to talk to Bim at night, because koalas sleep during the day!

• The Leadbetter's Possums in the mountains of Australia are really shy. But they warm up if you show them you're friendly. Try offering them a Cheese Treat. (But don't tell Darwin!)

• I know a Siberian tiger named Kalla. She's growing into an adult, so she likes hunting as much as she used to like playing! If you're visiting a tiger, and she happens to be hunting, don't sneak up and surprise her, or you could be her next dinner!

• Chimps in Africa will let you be their friend, as long as you follow their rules on how to talk to them— and there are lots of rules! I don't know how Darwin keeps them all straight. Maybe that's why he lives with us now!

DONNIE'S WORLD

On your travels, you'll meet all kinds of people. The best way to get to know them is talk to them. Let's practice with Donnie!

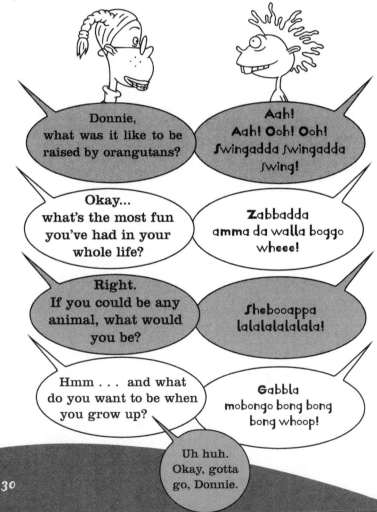

DEBBIE'S FASHION SCENE

Hey, it's not easy keeping up on the latest styles when your family keeps dragging you to Costa Del Somewhere or Mount Wherever. Have YOU ever tried finding a mall in the middle of the Serengeti Desert? Here's the gear you need if you're heading into the wilderness:

• Ripped jeans and flannel shirts: These are always in style no matter where you go!

• A handy vine makes a snappy belt for your jeans, and its green color will totally match a palm-frond hand fan.

- A parka for the Himalayas: Make sure it's not real fur, and try not to wear anything that clashes with the snow.

- Some pretty shells from the beaches of Australia: String them together for a way-cool necklace!

My family doesn't have the awesome fashion sense I do, but the stuff they wear does make a lot of sense.

Donnie's got that wild-man look that helps him blend in with any jungle, but I think a good pair of boots would make him the bomb.

Bandannas haven't been cool for, like, ever, but my mom can use hers as a rope to tie off our supplies, or as a mask to cover her mouth in a dust storm.

My sister thinks geek is chic. She's smart to travel with a backpack, but pigtails are totally out!

My dad thinks khaki is the only color in, like, the entire world. But his clothes have tons of pockets, which is great for keeping all the stuff you pick up when you're traveling!

Darwin's tank top probably keeps him cool, but *why bother*? He's a chimp!

GET THAT SHOT!

You have to be creative in solving problems when you're traveling. For example, taking great nature footage isn't always as easy as setting up the camera and pushing the "on" button! I've had to do some pretty strange things to make sure we got the pictures we needed, like . . .

• When I got sick, and we really needed to get footage of condors, I sent Debbie out to work the camera for me. She did a pretty good job—even if the final film was more like MTV than *Nigel Thornberry's Animal World*.

• Once, in order to get close enough to film turtles, we built our own shells to help us blend in among the turtles. Of course, Nigel got stuck in his shell.

• When I wanted film of an erupting volcano in the Galápagos Islands, Nigel was worried I'd stand too long in the path of the flowing lava. So he picked me up and I filmed as he ran! We got great footage!

NIGEL'S MUST-HAVES

Righty ho! Heading into the jungle to watch lemurs leap? Trekking into the Andes to see condors cavort? Either way, you'll need several things to make the journey pleasant and productive:

• Binoculars! Simply smashing for watching animals from a safe distance.

• A field guide, so you can be sure of what you're looking at: There's nothing more insulting to a short-tailed macaque than mistaking it for a long-tailed macaque! Good heavens, what a *faux pas* that would be!

• Kippers! A hike through the rain forest or sledding through the Arctic can be hungry work. Stoke your animal-enthusiast furnace with these fabulous fishies!

• Several small jars to collect samples of the local plant life: But it's not a good idea to collect samples of poison ivy—unless you're itching to do so! Ha ha!

• A bird call! One toot can bring even the most bashful of our feathered friends flocking to your side!

• A clean pair of boots! If you get invited to dine with the Yanomami, it's bad form to arrive in muddy puddle-jumpers!

• A guitar: Because there's nothing more relaxing on a nature hike than a chorus of your favorite cowboy ballad!

TROUBLE AHEAD!

If there's one thing I know how to do, it's how to spot trouble. And since I hang around with Eliza, I spot trouble *all* the time! So, take it from me . . .

• Avoid cobras! I met one in India, and he wasn't friendly at all! As a rule, I try to keep a big distance between me and anything with fangs!

• Don't be afraid to ask for directions. The world's a pretty big place, and there are lots of spots where you can get lost.

• Beware of strange recipes. I love a good dinner as much as the next chimp, but I don't like it when I'm scheduled to be the main course!

• Waterfalls are a lot more fun to look at when you're far away from them, than when you're about to go sailing over them!

• Listen to the local people when they tell you some place is dangerous. They should know—they live there and you don't!

• If you're going hiking, make sure you pick a trail with lots of nice, shady trees—preferably ones you can nap under with a coconut full of milk by your side!

THINK FAST

Not everything goes as planned when you're traveling around the world. Problems come up all the time. Here's what to do when . . .

You get caught by those nasty poachers, Kip and Beiderman:
Don't worry, because it shouldn't be too hard to escape. Those guys aren't very smart!

You meet up with a hungry or dangerous animal:
The first thing to do is talk to them. Of course, nobody but me can talk to animals, so the best thing for everyone else to do is to just back away . . . nice and slow.

You're caught in an avalanche:

Paddle your arms and keep your head above the snow. This will help you "surf" your way to the bottom of the mountain. Just pretend you're going for a really cold swim!

You come face to teeth with a shark:

Whack him on the nose. That's where he's most sensitive, and hopefully he'll swim away. If he doesn't, then you have to hope you can swim faster than he can!

A volcano erupts and lava starts to flow:

Drop everything and run! I don't care if you're carrying a chest full of gold coins. What good is gold when you're not around to spend it?

DEAR MR. CULPEPPER

Sometimes Mr. Culpepper, my home-schooling teacher, gets mad at me because I don't always do the homework assignment exactly the way he asks me to.

But that doesn't mean I haven't learned anything. I use lessons from school every day, and so will you . . .

Geometry:

I need to know what angle to use when I swing from tree to tree with Darwin!

English:

Knowing how my own language works helps me learn about the languages of the people we meet.

History:

My report on President Martin Van Buren came in handy! I rolled it up and used it as a breathing tube when I hid in a swamp!

Social Studies:

Animals are just like people. Have you ever spent a day watching a family of chimps? It's like watching your own family, only with more hair and bananas!

GORILLA IN THE MIDST

LOOK OUT, IT'S DONNIE!

Everybody likes Donnie. He's funny, friendly, and happy to try anything. But you have to be prepared for some of the things this wild child loves to do, like . . .

- **Eat:** Sometimes Donnie eats normal food, like my Cheese Treats. Other times, he'll eat bugs, leaves, dirt, rocks . . . in other words, just about anything!

- **Poke:** Donnie's happiest when he has something to poke! Sometimes it's not funny at all, like when he's poking me!

• **Run:** Donnie never walks anywhere! He always runs—and he's much faster than we are! If I ran like that all the time, I'd have to take lots of naps in the shade. Of course, I already like to do that . . .

• **Screech:** Donnie makes all kinds of noises, none of which anyone can understand! I thought chimps made a lot of noise, but Donnie makes a family of chimps sound like they're whispering!

• **Make a mess:** Donnie's better at doing this than anyone else in the whole world! You can spend the whole day cleaning the Commvee, but let Donnie inside for just a minute, and *poof!* Everything's a mess again!

IT'S THE BEST!

Yep, there are a lot of things to know when traveling. But it's worth it. I wouldn't trade traveling with my family for anything in the world!

To me, meeting new animals and making friends with them is the best thing about being on the road!

Every culture has its own popular music. After visiting so many cultures, my CD collection rules!

I'm always learning some-thing, and using the things I've learned before. That helps me make better and better movies!

Not many chimps can say they've seen what's outside their own jungle. With Eliza and her family, I get to discover something every day—and some of it isn't even dangerous!

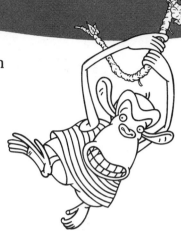

Exploring the wild is absolutely smashing—you never run out of things to see, places to go, or things to do. Nature never ceases to be a jolly good show. And what joy to be able to experience it all with my nearest and dearest close at hand!

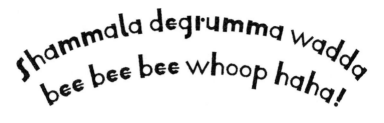

Shammala degrumma wadda bee bee bee whoop haha!